BENEFIT OF POSITIVITY
MAGIC OF OF POSITIVE LIVING

TABLE OF CONTENTS

CHAPTER 1: BEING DECISIVE

Decisiveness is key in many aspects of life. In business, being able to make quick, informed decisions can be the difference between success and failure. In personal relationships, being decisive can help prevent arguments and misunderstandings. And in general, being decisive can help you seize opportunities and achieve your goals.

Of course, being decisive doesn't mean always knowing exactly what to do. It's normal to feel uncertain at times. The key is to trust your instincts

and make the best decision you can based on the information you have.
If you're struggling to be decisive, there are a few things you can do to improve. First, try to become more aware of your own thought process. When you're feeling uncertain, what are you telling yourself? Second, practice making small decisions. The more you do it, the easier it will become. And finally, don't be afraid to ask for help when you need it. Sometimes other people can see things more clearly than we can, and they can be a valuable resource in making tough decisions.
In order to be successful in any field, it is essential to be decisive. Indecision can lead to missed opportunities and wasted time, both of which can be detrimental to your career. When you are presented with a decision to make, take the time to consider all of your options and then make a choice. Once you have made your decision, stick to it and don't second-guess yourself. Trusting your gut and being decisive will help you to achieve your goals.
When it comes to making decisions, it's important to be decisive. That means being able to weigh all the options and make a choice that you feel confident about. It can be difficult to be decisive, especially when there are a lot of options to consider. But being able to make decisions quickly and confidently is a valuable skill.
There are a few things you can do to help you be more decisive. First, try to get as much information as you can about all the options before you make a decision. Second, trust your gut. If

you have a strong feeling about one option, it's probably the right choice. Finally, don't be afraid to make a decision and then change your mind if you find out new information.

Making decisions can be tough, but by following these tips, you can become a more decisive person.

Making decisions can be hard, but it's important to be decisive in life. Indecisiveness can lead to missed opportunities and regret. It's essential to be able to weigh up pros and cons and then make a decision based on what you think is best. Trust your instincts and don't second-guess yourself – once you've made a decision, stick to it. Be confident in your choices and don't let others sway you. Remember, you're the only one who knows what's best for you, so make sure you're the one in charge of your life.

In order to be successful in any field, it is important to be decisive. This means being able to make quick and informed decisions, without second-guessing yourself. Of course, this is not always easy, and there will be times when you are unsure of what to do. However, overthinking things will only make the situation worse. Trust your instincts and go with your gut feeling. more often than not, you will find that you make the right decision.

There is no room for indecision in life. At every turn, we are faced with choices that require us to be decisive. Indecision is a luxury that we simply cannot afford.

In order to be successful in life, we must learn to make quick and effective decisions. This requires us to be well-informed and to have a clear understanding of our goals and objectives. We must also be confident in our ability to make the right choices.

indecision can lead to missed opportunities and wasted time. It can also lead to anxiety and stress. When we are indecisive, we are not in control of our lives. We are at the mercy of others who are more decisive than us.

So be decisive. Take control of your life. Make the choices that will lead you to success.

Making decisions can be difficult, but it's important to be decisive in order to move forward. When you're presented with a choice, take the time to consider your options and then make a decision. Once you've made a decision, stick to it and don't second-guess yourself. Trust that you made the right choice and move forward confidently. Being decisive will help you maintain progress and reach your goals.

CHAPTER 2: SELF CONFIDENCE

If you want to be successful in anything you do, you need to have self-confidence. This means having faith in your own abilities and being able to see yourself as a capable person. With self-confidence, you'll be able to take risks and go after your goals with determination. People who lack self-confidence often give up easily or don't even try in the first place. Don't let this be you! Develop your self-confidence by setting realistic goals for yourself and then taking small steps to achieve them. With each accomplishment, your self-confidence will grow and you'll be one step closer to success.

Self-confidence is an essential quality for success in any area of life. It's the inner belief that you can achieve anything you set your mind to. People who are self-confident know their strengths and weaknesses and are comfortable in their own skin. They don't compare themselves to others and don't let others define them.

Self-confident people are often successful in their chosen field, whether it's business, sports, or another area. They're able to take risks and bounce back from setbacks. They're also more likely to be happy and fulfilled in their personal lives.

If you want to be successful in any area of your life, start by developing your self-confidence. Set your sights high and believe in yourself. Surround yourself with positive people who will support your efforts. And don't be afraid to take risks. Remember, self-confidence is the key to success.

Self-confidence is one of the most important traits a person can have. It's the foundation of success in every area of life, from personal relationships to professional achievements. People who are self-confident exude an inner strength and peace that comes from knowing they can handle whatever life throws their way. They believe in themselves and their abilities, and they're able to stay calm and focused even in the face of adversity.

Self-confidence is not about being arrogant or thinking you're better than others. It's simply having a healthy belief in yourself and your abilities. It's the confidence that comes from knowing you have what it takes to succeed.

If you want to build self-confidence, start by setting realistic goals and then taking small, consistent steps to achieve them. Focus on your strengths and accomplishments, and learn to accept compliments and criticism alike. Remember that nobody is perfect, and that mistakes are part of the journey to success. Surround yourself with positive people who believe in you, and don't be afraid to step out of your comfort zone. With time and practice, you'll develop the self-confidence you need to reach your full potential.

Self-confidence is the belief in oneself and one's abilities. It is an important factor in success and happiness. People with high self-confidence are more likely to achieve their goals and be happier in life. They are also better able to cope with setbacks and overcome challenges.

Self-confidence is not the same as arrogance or narcissism. Arrogant people believe they are better than others and have a sense of entitlement. Narcissists are obsessed with themselves and their own needs. People with healthy self-confidence have a positive view of themselves and their abilities, but they also recognize that everyone has strengths and weaknesses.

Building self-confidence takes time and effort. It starts with accepting and valuing oneself, and then developing a realistic view of one's abilities. Setting small goals and achieving them can also help to increase self-confidence. Being around supportive and positive people can also make a big difference.

Self confidence is the belief in oneself and one's abilities. It is an essential quality for success in any field, and is especially important in leadership roles. A lack of self confidence can lead to self-doubt and a fear of failure, which can prevent people from taking risks and achieving their goals.

Self confidence is not something that can be learned overnight. It takes time and practice to develop. However, there are some things that everyone can do to start building self confidence. One of the most important things is to focus on positive self-talk. This means speaking kindly to oneself, and avoiding negative thoughts and words. It is also important to take care of oneself physically, by eating well and getting regular exercise. Finally, it is helpful to surround oneself with supportive people who will encourage and believe in one's abilities.

With time and effort, anyone can develop self confidence. It is a key ingredient for success in life, and is worth the investment.

Self confidence is the belief in oneself and one's abilities. It is the key to success in life. Without self confidence, we would not be able to achieve our goals. We would not be able to take risks or face challenges. We would not be able to pursue our dreams.

Self confidence is something that we all have within us. It is the belief that we can accomplish anything we set our minds to. It is the courage to take risks and the strength to overcome challenges. It is the determination to pursue our dreams.

Self confidence is the foundation of success. It is the belief in ourselves that allows us to take risks and face challenges. It is the courage to pursue our dreams. By developing self confidence, we can achieve anything we set our minds to.

Self confidence is the belief in oneself and one's ability to succeed. It is an essential quality for success in any field, and is especially important in difficult or challenging situations. Self confidence can be developed through positive thinking, practice, and constructive feedback from others. It is a key ingredient in success at work, in relationships, and in other areas of life.

Self-confidence is the belief in oneself and one's ability to succeed. It is an important factor in achieving success in any area of life. People who are self-confident are more likely to take risks and seize opportunities. They are also better able to cope with setbacks and failure.

Self-confidence is not the same as arrogance or narcissism. Arrogant people believe they are better than others and have no need for improvement. Narcissists are obsessed with their own image and believe they can do no wrong. Both of these types of people are usually disliked by others.

Self-confident people are generally more successful and happier than those who lack confidence. They are also more likely to be liked and respected by others. If you want to achieve success in any area of your life, it is important to develop self-confidence.

Self confidence is the belief in oneself that one can cope with any situation and achieve anything. It is the foundation of success in life. People with self confidence are positive and optimistic and have a can-do attitude. They are also able to face challenges and setbacks with courage and determination.

Self confidence is not something that you are born with, it is something that you develop over time. You can start building your self confidence by setting yourself small goals and then achieving them. As you start to accomplish more, your self confidence will grow. Remember, there is no limit to what you can achieve if you believe in yourself!

CHAPTER 3: HAVING GOOD ENERGY

TOWARDS OTHERS

The ability to have good energy towards others is essential for success in any field. It is the ability to be positive and enthusiastic about working with or around others. This trait is especially important in customer service, sales, and any job that requires close interaction with others. Good energy is also essential for maintaining healthy personal and professional relationships. When we have good energy towards others, we are more likely to be successful in any endeavor.

Energy is everything. It's the force that drives us forward and allows us to interact with the world around us. Good energy is positive, optimistic, and enthusiastic. It's the kind of energy that makes us feel good about ourselves and others. bad energy is negative, pessimistic, and cynical. It's the kind of energy that makes us feel bad about ourselves and others. Good energy is contagious, and it's something we should all strive to have. When we have good energy towards others, it creates a positive feedback loop that can make the world a better place. So let's all try to have more good energy towards others, and see what happens!

When we have good energy towards others, it means that we are thinking, speaking and acting in ways that are positive and helpful. We might be smiling more, offering compliments or support, and generally just trying to make things better for the people around us. Good energy is contagious, and it can make a big difference in the overall atmosphere of any situation. It's also a great way to build relationships and create positive interactions.

When we are happy and at peace with ourselves, we naturally exude positive energy. Other people can feel this and are naturally drawn to us. On the other hand, when we are angry, resentful or unhappy, we give off negative energy which repels other people.

Good energy is not just about being happy all the time, though. It's also about having a positive attitude towards others, even when they may be difficult to deal with. If we can see the good in others, even when they are behaving badly, we are more likely to be able to find common ground and connect with them.

It's not always easy to have good energy towards others, but it's definitely worth the effort. When we do, we create a more positive and harmonious world for everyone.

Having good energy towards others is one of the most important things that you can do in life. It not only makes you a better person, but it also makes the world a better place. When you have good energy towards others, you are automatically putting out positive vibes into the universe. These positive vibes then come back to you, and the cycle continues. It's a beautiful thing.

It is always a good idea to have good energy towards others. When we have good energy, it helps to attract good things into our lives. It also helps to create positive interactions with the people we come into contact with. Good energy is also contagious, so when we are surrounded by people with good energy, it can help to improve our mood and outlook on life. Having good energy towards others is important for a variety of reasons. For one, it can help build strong relationships with others. Good energy can also make others feel more comfortable and safe around you. Additionally, having good energy can make you more likely to succeed in your endeavors, whether personal or professional. Finally, good energy towards others can simply make the world a better place. When you have good energy, you radiate positivity and good vibes, which can have a ripple effect on those around you. So next time you're interacting with others, be sure to check your energy level and make sure you're putting your best foot forward.

When we have good energy towards others, it means that we are radiating positive vibes and good will. This is contagious, and often results in the person we are interacting with also feeling good. This is the best way to create positive relationships with others, whether it be in our personal lives or in our professional lives. When we are kind, patient, and good-natured with others, they are more likely to reciprocate these qualities. This creates a positive feedback loop of good energy that can benefit everyone involved.

Having good energy towards others is very important. It can make the difference between having a good day and having a bad day. Good energy is contagious, and it can make others around you feel better as well. It's also important to be aware of your own energy levels and make sure that you're not putting out too much or too little. Too much energy can be overwhelming, and too little can make you seem uninterested. Finding the right balance is key to having good energy towards others.

Having good energy towards others is important for many reasons. For one, it helps create positive relationships and interactions with others. Good energy also makes you more likely to be successful in your endeavors, whether they are personal or professional. Finally, good energy towards others simply makes you a more pleasant person to be around, which can lead to all sorts of other positive benefits.

When we interact with others, it's important to project positive energy. This can be done in many ways, such as maintaining eye contact, smiling, and speaking in a clear and friendly tone of voice. Good energy is contagious, so by exuding it ourselves, we can help create a more positive environment for everyone around us. Additionally, when we approach others with good energy, they are more likely to respond positively to us in return. This can help build strong relationships and foster a sense of community. So next time you're interacting with someone,

remember to put your best foot forward and show them some good energy!
Having good energy towards others is important for a variety of reasons. First, it creates a positive atmosphere and sets the tone for interactions. When we have good energy towards others, it is contagious and helps create a more positive world for everyone. Additionally, good energy is simply more pleasant to be around. It makes people feel good and is a sign of a kind and caring person. Finally, good energy is a sign of respect. When we have good energy towards others, we are respecting them as fellow human beings and valuing them as such. This is an important part of creating a more peaceful and just world.

CHAPTER:4

PRACTICALIZE YOUR THOUGHTS AND DREAMS

It is often said that we should practicalize our thoughts and dreams in order to achieve success. While this may be true to some extent, we should also remember that our thoughts and dreams are what give us the motivation and inspiration to achieve our goals. Without them, we would be like robots, going through the motions without any passion or purpose.

So while it is important to be practical and to have a plan, we should also allow ourselves to dream big and to think creatively. We should not be afraid to take risks and to think outside the box. Only by doing this will we be able to achieve great things and to make our dreams a reality.

There's no better time than now to start practicalizing your thoughts and dreams. Whether it's getting your dream job, traveling the world, or simply becoming a better person, there's no time like the present to start making your dreams a reality.

The first step is to clearly define what it is you want to achieve. Once you have a clear goal in mind, you can start making a plan to achieve it. This may involve saving money, learning new skills, or networking with people who can help you achieve your goal. Whatever it is you want to achieve, remember that it's important to take actionable steps towards your goal. Don't let your dreams remain just dreams - make them happen!

You can practicalize your thoughts and dreams by taking small steps towards your goals. You can start by writing down your thoughts and dreams, and then you can start working on a plan to make them a reality. You can also talk to people who have similar goals and see how they have achieved them. You can also look for resources that can help you practicalize your thoughts and dreams.

There's no time like the present to practicalize your thoughts and dreams. If you've been thinking about making a change in your life, now is the time to act on it. If you've been dreaming about starting your own business, now is the time to start putting your plans into action.

The bottom line is that if you want to make something happen, you have to take action. Dreams and thoughts are wonderful, but they won't amount to anything if you don't do something with them. So get out there and start making your dreams a reality!

No matter how big or small, our thoughts and dreams are what make us who we are. They give us something to strive for and keep us going when things get tough. But it's not enough to just have big dreams – we need to practicalize them too.

Think about what you want to achieve and what steps you need to take to get there. Create a plan and set yourself some achievable goals. And most importantly, don't be afraid to take risks and seize opportunities when they arise.

Practicalizing our thoughts and dreams is the only way to turn them into reality. So let's get started and make our dreams come true!

Your thoughts and dreams are the foundation of your future success. If you can't practicalize them, they'll never become a reality. But what exactly does it mean to practicalize your thoughts and dreams?

It means turning them into actionable steps that you can take to make your dreams come true. It means setting goals and making a plan to achieve them. And it means being relentless in your pursuit of your goals, never giving up no matter how difficult things get.

If you want to be successful, you have to start by practicalizing your thoughts and dreams. Only then can you hope to turn them into a reality.

There's no better feeling than knowing you're on the right track in life. All your hard work is finally paying off and you're finally starting to see the fruits of your labor. But as you start to get closer to your goals, you may start to feel like you're in a rut. You've been working so hard and for so long, but you're not quite sure how to make your dreams a reality.

The key is to practicalize your thoughts and dreams. Start by taking a step back and looking at your goals. What are your long-term goals? What are your short-term goals? What steps do you need to take to achieve these goals? Once you have a clear plan, it's time to start taking action.

Start small. Don't try to do everything at once. Focus on one goal at a time and break it down into smaller pieces. For example, if your goal is to start your own business, break it down into smaller steps like writing a business plan, finding funding, and marketing your business.

As you start to take action and make progress, you'll start to see your dreams become a reality. It takes time and effort, but it's so worth it when you finally achieve your goals. So don't give up and keep working towards your dreams.

Dreams are the cornerstone of human motivation. They are the engine that drives us to achieve great things. But all too often, our dreams remain just that: dreams. We never take the steps to turn them into reality.
It doesn't have to be this way. You can practicalize your dreams and make them a reality. It starts with a change in mindset. Instead of seeing your dreams as unattainable, view them as challenges to be overcome. Break them down into smaller goals and take actionable steps to achieve them.
You will also need to develop a thick skin. Pursuing your dreams will not be easy. You will face obstacles and criticism. But if you stay focused on your goals and believe in yourself, you will eventually achieve them.
So don't let your dreams remain dreams. Practicalize them and make them a reality. It's the only way to achieve true greatness.

CHAPTER 5: SELF-CONTENTEMENT

When you're content with yourself, you don't need validation from others. You're confident in your own skin and you don't compare yourself to others. You know your worth and you don't let anyone else tell you otherwise. You're happy with who you are and you don't feel the need to change for anyone.
Being content with oneself is a trait that many people lack. In today's

society, people are constantly comparing themselves to others and feeling inadequate. This leads to feelings of insecurity and low self-esteem. Learning to be content with oneself is an important step in developing positive self-esteem. It means accepting oneself for who they are and not compare oneself to others. It also means being thankful for what one has and not wanting more than what is necessary. Achieving self contentment is the key to positivity. Once you are content with who you are, what you have, and where you are in life, everything else falls into place. You stop caring about what other people think of you and start living your life for yourself. This doesn't mean that you become selfish, but rather that you focus on your own happiness. When you are content with yourself, you are more likely to be happy and to radiate positive energy. Being content with oneself is a trait not many people have. Being content with what you have, who you are, and where you're at in life is one of the most important things to focus on. It's not about having more than others, it's about being happy with what you have. Once you're able to do that, everything else will fall into place. You'll be able to better deal with the negativity in the world and be a more positive person overall

THE IMPORTANCE OF CONTENTMENT

It’s almost impossible to stress enough how important it is to be content. The importance of contentment is outlined below. Some benefits of contentment include:

Peace of mind

Contentment brings peace of mind and positivity that can facilitate growth and self-improvement. This does not mean you can't have dreams and aspirations. You can accept the present and still wish for a better future. Contentment only means to be at peace with the present, not complacent.

If you are not at peace with what you have achieved at your current point in life, it can be more difficult be motivated to work toward a better future. If you want peace of mind and a positive attitude, contentment is what you should practice.

Happiness

Contentment promotes happiness. When you are content with the present, you are letting go of sometimes painful cravings for what you can't have. As a result, acceptance settles in. Therefore, when you accept your situation, you are allowing yourself to be happy. Being grateful for everything you do have instead of spending most of your time thinking about what you can't have could make life a lot more beautiful.

Stronger relationships

When you allow yourself to be content, you are also telling yourself to accept others as they are. The benefits of contentment are not limited to your own well-being; they can also encompass relationships. (This does not extend to abusive relationships, however.)

Accepting others, including their flaws, and being content with the present may fuel feelings of happiness and prosperity in relationships, making them stronger. It can enrich relationships with trust and appreciation as well as promote healing and growth.

Distinguishing wants and needs

Contentment can help you distinguish between wants and needs. When you are content, you may not desire for anything more than what you need. The abundance of the present is enough to lead a happy and healthy life. Contentment often leads to the realization that joy doesn't come from material things. Instead, joy comes from deep within.

Simplicity

When you are able to distinguish your wants from your needs, you stop overburdening yourself. You relieve yourself from the stress of wanting more and more. Contentment promotes simplicity. It teaches you to be happy with what you have, whether little or abundant.

Instead of wanting your possessions to grow, you start working on personal growth. Because at the end of the day, inner peace fueled by contentment may matter more than the car you drive or even the house you live in.

If you wish to feel the essence of contentment, it's important to practice gratitude, be aware of the fact that nothing is permanent, understand that material things do not often promote long-term happiness, and realize that life is not a race or competition: it is about self-sustenance. The more thankful you are in the present, the happier you may be.

CHAPTER 6: BE FOCUSED

In order to be positive, it is important to be focused. This means setting goals and working towards them. It also means being mindful of your thoughts and emotions, and choosing to focus on the good. Additionally, being focused also means staying present in the moment and savoring the good things that are happening right now. When you are focused, you are more likely to be positive.

It is important to stay focused on what is positive in your life. This means not dwelling on the negative things that happen, but instead choosing to focus on the good. When you do this, you will find that your outlook on life improves and that you are able to better enjoy the good moments. You may also find that you are better able to handle the bad moments when they do occur.

Being focused is the key to success in any area of your life. If you want to be successful, you need to focus on your goals and put all of your effort into achieving them. Being positive and optimistic will also help you to stay on track. When you have a positive outlook, you are more likely to see opportunities and possibilities instead of obstacles.

Positivity is something that can be practiced. It's the act of being aware of your own thoughts and making a conscious effort to focus on the positive. This doesn't mean ignoring the negative, but it does mean giving more attention to the things that make you feel good. When you focus on positive thoughts, you'll start to see more positive results in your life.

Eliminate distractions

You will be more productive and have a better chance of staying focused when you remove anything in your surroundings that might cause interruptions. If feasible, try keeping your phone in a different room or staying offline to minimize distractions and improve your focus overall. Working alone or in a quiet environment will also make you more focused.

Prioritize your tasks

If you have a lengthy number of tasks to complete, it can be beneficial to not only create a to-do list, but to also rank each item by its level of importance. This lets you focus on one task at a time, allowing you to methodically work through your tasks instead of simply being overwhelmed and likely ineffectual.

Train your mind

Engaging in various brain training activities is a great way to improve your cognitive abilities and subsequently, your ability to stay focused. When you instruct your brain to become more disciplined, you can become more active in paying attention to the task in front of you.

Focus Exercises for Improving Concentration Skills

Work in a quiet space

When you're working alone or in a secluded area, you're more apt to get more work done. A quiet environment can help you improve your focus as it ensures you won't be interrupted by colleagues or other noisy distractions from your workplace environment.

Try meditation

Taking the time to relax, breathe and meditate can greatly improve your cognitive abilities, including mental focus and concentration. Try practicing yoga to strengthen your ability to concentrate in the workplace.

Exercise

Exercising regularly stimulates your brain and keeps it refreshed. Engaging in physical activity will also improve memory capacity and overall concentration. Not only will it help you stay energized, but it'll also give you the extra boost you need to stay focused and on task at work.

Take breaks

Taking time for yourself is a great way to avoid burnout. While steadily completing tasks is important, giving your mind time to recharge and relax can be greatly beneficial for your mental health. If you're stuck on a task, walking away for a short while can provide you with a fresh perspective. Taking a break and allowing your brain time to shut down can also provide you with the momentum you need when you return to work and improve your focus on the task at hand.

Get a good night's sleep

Sleeping at least eight hours a night is a great way to make sure you're in your best physical and mental state when you arrive at work. Being sleepy causes you to slow down. Getting a good night's rest, on the other hand, allows you to remain alert and awake—especially during the morning hours.

Focus on one thing at a time

When you direct your attention toward one sole task, your risk of distraction minimizes. Rather than multitasking, keep your brain actively engaged on one thing at a time. Improve your quality of work and your attention span by focusing on one task first, then moving onto the next.

Brain Hacks for When You Can't Focus at Work

Allot time to certain tasks

When determining what tasks you need to complete, consider the length of time you'll need to complete each. Scheduling out your day and exercising your time management skills will help you complete your work more efficiently and help you stay on top of it all. For example, allot 8-10 a.m. to complete task one, 10-11 a.m. to complete task two and so forth.

Learning how to focus by applying helpful tactics to improve your attention span can help you become a better employee. Though distractions are bound to arise, learning how to deal with them as well as determining what will work well for you, are great starting points to consider.

CHAPTER 7: SELF DISCIPLINE

self discipline
Attitude is defined as the way you dedicate yourself to the way you think. Think negative or think positive is a choice and a process. Negative is (unfortunately) an instinctive process. Positive is a learned self-discipline that must be studied and practiced every day.
Avoid acting rashly and impulsively.
Carry out the promises and decisions you make to yourself and to others.
Break bad habits.
Make wise and healthy choices.
Overcome the tendency to laziness and procrastination.
Improve your ability to concentrate and stay focused when working, reading or studying.
Continue working on a project, even after the initial rush of enthusiasm has faded away.
Exercising, going for a walk, or hitting the gym.
Continue working on your diet, and resisting the temptation of eating fattening foods.
It will give you the inner strength to get out of bed in the morning promptly, even if it is cold.
Overcome the habit of watching too much TV.
You will meet your tasks and goals confidently and pursue them assiduously.

Accomplishing even just a small part of this list is a great achievement, which can have positive effects on your life

Set clear goals and have an execution plan.

If you hope to achieve greater degrees of self-discipline, you must have a clear vision of what you hope to accomplish, just like any goal. You must also have an understanding of what success means to you. After all, if you don't know where you are going, it's easy to lose your way or get sidetracked. Remember to prioritize. At TakingPoint Leadership, when we work with our corporate clients on strategic planning, execution, and organizational transformation, we remind them that having ten priorities translates to no priorities.

A clear plan outlines each time-bound step you must take to reach your goals. Create a mantra to keep yourself focused. Successful people use this technique to stay on track, emotionally connect to their mission, and establish a clear finish line.

Practice daily diligence.

We aren't born with self-discipline; it's a learned behavior. And just like any other skill you want to master, it requires daily practice and repetition. It must become habitual. But the effort and focus that self-discipline requires can be draining. As time passes, it can become more and more difficult to keep your willpower in check. The bigger the temptation or decision, the more challenging it can feel to tackle other tasks that also require self-control.

So, work on building your self-discipline through daily diligence in a given area associated with a goal. This goes back to step three. In order to practice daily diligence, you must have a plan. Put it on your calendar, your to-do list, tattoo it on the back of your eyelids - whatever works best for you. With practice, anyone can push the boundaries of their comfort zone every day.

Create new habits and rituals.

Acquiring self-discipline and working to instill a new habit can feel daunting at first, especially if you focus on the entire task at hand. To avoid feeling intimidated, keep it simple. Break your goal into small, doable steps. Instead of trying to change everything at once, focus on doing one thing consistently and master self-discipline with that goal in mind.

As we say in the SEAL Teams, "Eat the elephant one bite at a time."

If you're trying to get in shape but don't exercise regularly (or ever), start by working out ten or fifteen minutes a day. If you're trying to achieve better sleep habits, start by going to bed thirty minutes earlier each night. If you want to eat healthier, change your grocery shopping habits and prep meals ahead of time. Take baby steps. Eventually, when your mindset and behavior starts to shift, you can add more goals to your list.

Change your perception about willpower.

If you believe you have a limited amount of willpower, you probably won't surpass those limits. As I mentioned previously, studies show that willpower can deplete over time. But what about changing that perception? The SEAL candidate who believes they probably won't make it through training won't succeed. Why assume our will to win can only take us so far?

When we embrace the mindset of unlimited willpower, we continue to grow, achieve more, and develop mental toughness. It's the same philosophy as setting "stretch" goals. In short, our internal conceptions about willpower and self-control can determine how disciplined we are. If you can remove these subconscious obstacles and truly believe you can do it, then you will give yourself an extra boost of motivation toward making those goals a reality.

Give yourself a backup plan.

In the SEAL Teams, we always have contingency plans. Psychologists use a technique to boost willpower called "implementation intention." That's when you give yourself a plan to deal with a potentially difficult situation you know you will likely face. To be clear, I am not referring to a backup plan under the auspices that you'll probably fail at Plan A.

Let's say you aspire to become a trapeze expert, but tell yourself, "Well, I'm probably not going to excel at this, so chances are I'll be sticking with miniature golf." That's a lame backup plan wrapped in mediocrity. We are talking about contingencies for intentional course correction, not planning for failure. So be bold and keep moving forward. Going in with a plan will help give you the mindset and self-control necessary for the situation. You will also save energy by not having to make a sudden decision based on your emotional state.

Find trusted coaches or mentors. The development of expertise requires coaches who are capable of giving constructive, even painful, feedback. Real experts are extremely motivated students who seek out such feedback. They're also skilled at understanding when and if a coach or mentor's advice doesn't work for them.

The elite performers I've known and worked with always knew what they were doing right while concentrating on what they were doing wrong. They deliberately picked unsentimental coaches who would challenge them and drive them to higher levels of performance. The best coaches also identify aspects of your performance that will need to be improved at your next level of skill and aid you in preparation.

Forgive yourself and move forward. Even with all our best intentions and well laid plans, we sometimes fall short. It happens. You will have ups and downs, great successes and dismal failures. The key is to keep going. A very close SEAL buddy of mine has had a lifelong dream of not just serving in the SEAL Teams but also making it to our tier one special missions unit. He has every qualification this unit could possibly want, but for some reason they didn't select him on his first application attempt. Did he wallow in sorrow? Not for one second. He immediately developed a plan to request even more "schools," train even harder, and he transferred to a different SEAL Team for a better chance to get picked up next time. Easy day.

If you stumble, find the root cause by asking the five WHY's and move on. Don't let yourself get wrapped up in guilt, anger, or frustration, because these emotions will only drag you further down and impede future progress.

SUMMARY: It has been scientifically proven that maintaining a positive outlook on life can lead to increased levels of happiness and better overall health. When you are positive, your body releases endorphins, which have mood-boosting and pain-relieving properties. Additionally, positivity can help protect you from the harmful effects of stress.

Positive thinking has also been linked to improved heart health, lower blood pressure, and increased life expectancy. So, not only can being positive make you feel better mentally, it can also have physical benefits.

If you are struggling to maintain a positive outlook, there are a few things you can do to help yourself. Spend time with positive people, do things you enjoy, and make an effort to see the good in every situation. With a little effort, you can reap the many benefits of positivity.

Positivity has a number of benefits that can help improve our lives in many ways. For one, positive thinking can help increase our productivity and motivation. When we focus on the good, we are more likely to work harder and achieve our goals.

Additionally, positivity can also lead to better physical health. Studies have shown that people who think positively tend to have lower levels of stress and anxiety, which can boost immunity and lead to better overall health. Finally, positivity can also improve our relationships. When we are positive and optimistic, we are more likely to attract and maintain healthy relationships.

www.ingramcontent.com/pod-product-compliance
Lightning Source LLC
LaVergne TN
LVHW052112160826
845678LV00015B/3500

* 9 7 9 8 8 4 9 7 7 3 0 5 6 *